The 7 Laws of Stress Management

The 7 Laws of Stress Management

Life-Changing Strategies for Maintaining Balance in Your Personal and Professional Life

Anthony D. Parnell, M.S.W.
Author of *Healing through Writing, Mind Games* and *In Search of Soul*

iUniverse, Inc.
New York Lincoln Shanghai

The 7 Laws of Stress Management
Life-Changing Strategies for Maintaining Balance in Your Personal and Professional Life

Copyright © 2008 by Anthony D. Parnell

All rights reserved. No part of this book may be used or reproduced by any means, graphic, electronic, or mechanical, including photocopying, recording, taping or by any information storage retrieval system without the written permission of the publisher except in the case of brief quotations embodied in critical articles and reviews.

iUniverse books may be ordered through booksellers or by contacting:

iUniverse
2021 Pine Lake Road, Suite 100
Lincoln, NE 68512
www.iuniverse.com
1-800-Authors (1-800-288-4677)

Because of the dynamic nature of the Internet, any Web addresses or links contained in this book may have changed since publication and may no longer be valid.

ISBN: 978-0-595-45660-4 (pbk)
ISBN: 978-0-595-89962-3 (ebk)

Printed in the United States of America

The views expressed in this work are solely those of the author and do not necessarily reflect the views of the publisher, and the publisher hereby disclaims any responsibility for them.

Cover Design by Joshua Lewis

Edited by Stephen Silke

This book is dedicated to all of my friends and family who have supported my vision and my personal quest for balance and well-being in my personal and professional life.

Contents

Introduction xi
The Concept of Balance and Well-Being xiii
The Concept of Stress xxi

PART I: THE 7 LAWS OF STRESS MANAGEMENT

Law Number 1: Stress Management is a Lifestyle that Requires an Individual to be Proactive Rather than Reactive 3

Law Number 2: Every Individual Needs an Adequate Amount of Time Alone and Silence to Maintain Balance in His Daily Life 7

Law Number 3: Honesty with Oneself is Essential 11

Law Number 4: Developing Greater Self-Awareness is Required to Maintain Balance in One's Personal and Professional Life 15

Law Number 5: Balance Can be Achieved Only When There is an Equal Commitment to One's Mind, Body and Spirit 19

Law Number 6: Developing Realistic Expectations Allows an Individual to Set Realistic Goals 23

Law Number 7: Long-Term Change Requires Discipline, Patience and a Commitment to the Daily Process of Maintaining Balance 28

PART II: 7 STEPS TO DEVELOPING AND IMPLEMENTING AN EFFECTIVE STRESS MANAGEMENT PLAN

Step Number 1: Declutter One's Thoughts and Emotions 35

Step Number 2: Identify Warning Signs & Stressors 39

Step Number 3: Develop Prioritized Stress Management Goals 49

Step Number 4: Identify Internal and External Resources..................... 63

Step Number 5: Declutter One's Physical Environment 69

Step Number 6: Surround Oneself with Positive People, Places and Things 77

Step Number 7: "Putting It All Together" 80

Appendix A: Self-Exploratory Questions... 85

Appendix B: Maintenance Plan for Decluttering Thoughts 87

Appendix C: Stress in the Workplace Grading Charts.......................... 89

Appendix D: Weekly and Monthly Extracurricular Activity Chart 93

Appendix E: Stress Management Goals Chart...................................... 97

Appendix F: Maintenance Plan for Decluttering Environment............ 99

Appendix G: Self-Care Monitoring Chart 103

Additional Resources 109

References... 111

Empowerment Workshops 113

Introduction

The Concept of Balance and Well-Being

The benefits of writing and self-reflection I have experienced in my personal life, for sixteen years, have significantly contributed to the idea of structuring *The Seven Laws of Stress Management* in a workbook format. This is combined with more than a decade of professional experience as a mental health therapist and workshop facilitator, helping others identify and utilize healthy methods for coping with stress and maintaining balance in their personal and professional lives. The emotional and spiritual benefits of writing and self-reflection on a daily or consistent basis are described in detail in my book, *Healing through Writing: A Journaling Guide to Emotional and Spiritual Growth* (2005). *Healing through Writing* also presents examples of various methods of journal writing, techniques for developing greater self-awareness, and a self-inventory tool for monitoring emotional and spiritual growth through what I call, "Seven Determinants of Emotional and Spiritual Growth".

The *Seven Laws of Stress Management* is an extension of the philosophy and techniques of *Healing through Writing* in that it provides a step-by-step approach to expanding self-awareness and maintaining balance and well-being. Empowering individuals to maintain balance in their personal and professional lives, *The Seven Laws of Stress Management* offers a framework for viewing balance as a multi-dimensional element of our human make-up (mind, body and spirit) and personal growth as a continuous cycle fueled by an individual's level of commitment.

My personal and professional experiences have affirmed that the ability to maintain balance and well-being in an individual's personal and professional life is a skill acquired over time. One, therefore, does not simply read a book to learn how to maintain balance and well-being. Rather, one must make a conscious commitment to developing the discipline to incorporate a routine of consistent self-reflection and other rituals into his or her daily life and adopting holistic beliefs that encompass an awareness of mind, body and spirit.

The Seven Laws of Stress Management workbook is designed to challenge you to commit to writing and self-exploration on a daily basis as a means to effectively managing stress and facilitating personal growth. Ultimately, *The Seven Laws of Stress Management* provides a roadmap for developing and maintaining a proactive lifestyle that promotes balance and well-being.

Part I begins with an outline and description of seven laws or guidelines for maintaining a balanced lifestyle. You are encouraged to examine strengths and weaknesses in your lifestyle—habits of daily living—as it relates to each of these seven laws. More specifically, you are encouraged to write your thoughts, emotions and life experiences that relate to each of the seven laws as a means of gaining greater clarity in your beliefs and in your ability to identify internal and external obstacles to achieving balance and well-being in daily life. For you to maximize the benefits of this book, you must concurrently record your thoughts, emotions and reflections in a journal or spiral notebook.

Part II provides a seven-step process for developing, implementing and maintaining an effective stress management plan. This section begins by challenging you to commit to decluttering your thoughts and emotions through the implementation of brief daily or consistent journaling to prevent the build up of negative energy and emotional clutter in your personal and professional life. Later in this section, the importance of decluttering your physical environment is emphasized in an effort to create space, organization and positive energy in your physical surroundings. Part II continues with the identification of warning signs and stressors as part of the process of formulating written "Prioritized Stress Management Goals." The book concludes with the final step of the seven-step process, "Putting It All Together," where the reader is reminded that a sustained level of commitment is the most essential ingredient to ensuring one's success in minimizing stress and encouraged to refer, as often as needed, to any part of *The 7 Laws of Stress Management* in the future.

The Seven Laws of Stress Management is rooted in the philosophy that balance and well-being can only be achieved and maintained when the needs of one's mind, body and spirit are adequately addressed. Your physical, mental and spiritual states of existence, from day to day, are interconnected. Thus, your physical condition should not be given greater emphasis than your mental or spiritual condition as an indicator of health, balance and well-being. Equally, a high level of self-awareness is required to identify and eliminate barriers to achieving and maintaining a state of mental, physical and spiritual harmony.

The Seven Laws of Stress Management is a philosophical and practical guide to achieving and maintaining balance in your daily life. To fully utilize the principles, concepts, and techniques presented in this book, you must commit to the daily discipline of silence and meditation that is required to become more in tune with your mind, body and spirit. Not only can you ascertain a greater understanding and awareness of the interconnectedness of your mind, body and spirit through this book, but you will also identify seven key principles for daily living to guide your thought processes, behavior and patterns of decision-making. In addition, you will gain a greater sense of enlightenment, and be empowered to develop and implement daily habits of living to foster growth, balance and well-being in your personal and professional life.

DEFINITIONS

Definitions for seven key words that are closely related to the concept of balance and well-being are listed below. As you read each definition, one at a time, take a few moments to reflect on each word. Also, in an effort to reinforce your understanding of each of the seven key words, space has been provided on the following pages to record any life experiences, thoughts or emotions that may be triggered or related to the definitions, and the concept of maintaining balance and well-being. This serves as an opportunity to make your initial entry in your journal.

STRESS—*The nonspecific response of the body to any demand, whether it is caused by, or results in, pleasant or unpleasant conditions* (Hans Selye, *The Stress of Life*, page 74).

BALANCE—*The ability to achieve and sustain empowerment to cope with the predictable and unpredictable demands of one's personal and professional life; the inner and outer work that an individual puts forth to achieve and sustain a consistent flow of positive energy in one's daily life* (Anthony D. Parnell, *Healing Through Writing*, 2005).

SELF-AWARENESS—*The ability of an individual to assess the potential impact of life stressors on one's well-being such that one simultaneously is able to identify internal and external resources available to minimize the damage to one's mind, body and spirit; the ability to independently explore and understand the source of one's thoughts, emotions, and behavior* (Anthony D. Parnell, *Healing Through Writing*, 2005).

EMPOWERMENT—*The ability of an individual to identify and to consistently utilize the Internal and External Resources that have been identified to improve one's life situation and to maintain balance and well-being in one's personal and professional life* (Anthony D. Parnell, *Healing Through Writing*, 2005).

SPIRITUALITY—*One's awareness of the Universal Life Force that creates and sustains all living things and one's ability to utilize this awareness to grow in love, expand consciousness, and to fulfill one's life purpose* (Anthony D. Parnell, *Healing Through Writing*, 2005).

HEALING—*The process of restoring balance to one's mind, body and spirit; addressing unmet physical, emotional and spiritual needs* (Anthony D. Parnell, *Healing Through Writing*, 2005).

WHOLENESS—*An individual's ability to effectively process one's thoughts and emotions and to respond effectively to life situations and to others without being limited by gender, race, age and so on ...* (Anthony D. Parnell, *Healing Through Writing*, 2005).

Personal Reflection

Personal Reflection

The Concept of Stress

The complexity of the phenomenon of stress can be evidenced by the myriad of life challenges with which we must contend on a daily basis – financial challenges, family and work demands and so on. Even more, the culture of our modern society has evolved such that we are bombarded and frequently overwhelmed by the daily demands for time and energy that are placed on us.

According to a 2007 natural survey conducted by the American Psychological Association (APA, www.apahelpcenter.mediaroom.com, 2007) "… nearly half of all Americans report that stress has a negative impact on both their personal and professional lives." More than 50 % report physical symptoms (fatigue; headache; upset stomach) and psychological symptoms (experiencing irritability or anger; feeling nervous; lack of energy) related to stress in the last month. And, for three-quarters of Americans, money and work are the leading causes of stress.

Stress is common to everyone, personally and professionally, but we experience and respond to life situations in our own unique way. While the birth of a child, for some, induces tremendous financial and emotional strain, for others, it provides a sense of spiritual joy and fulfillment, despite the financial and emotional sacrifice. This is the irony of stress in that it has its negative as well as its positive qualities, and its impact varies from person to person.

The broad scope of stress makes the concept of "balance" and "self-awareness" so significant. Stress, while having the potential to cause great damage to your mind, body and spirit also is an essential characteristic for strengthening an your mental, physical and spiritual self. Hence, stress is an intrinsic life force of nature. A body builder cannot develop a muscular physique without adding "stress" or tension to the muscles in the body through constant repetition and the systematic application of pressure and weight. This is combined with the understanding of knowing how much rest to give the body during and after workouts so that the body has time to properly heal. Yet, in the same instance, an individual who over exerts his or her self by lifting too much weight before the body has developed enough strength and flexibility will bring harm to the body rather than make it stronger. A sculptured physique is the end result of learning how to exercise discipline and how to be more in tune with the body.

There are numerous examples of the delicate balance that must be maintained within your daily life to promote growth and oppose deterioration. Sunlight, food and water are all vital to existence. At the same time, they also require a balance in their intake and consumption to ensure that equilibrium is maintained within the body and to allow the body to perform at optimal levels. Thus, the analogy of the body builder is also true within your mental and spiritual self. For everything, there is a threshold at which there is over-consumption or under-consumption. While there must be an exertion of force for growth to occur, constant self-awareness must also be maintained from moment to moment in order to adequately address the ever changing needs of your mind, body and spirit. Your ultimate challenge in minimizing stress is learning to manage the shifts of mental, physical and spiritual energy that you experience in your everyday life. In many ways, effective stress management can be viewed as a balancing act of learning how and when to consistently replace the negative energy in your life with positive energy.

There are volumes of literature and scientific research on the causes and effects of stress. Most notably, Hans Selye, M.D. through his scientific research of the causes of stress and the physical reactions of the body to stress, developed the concept of the *General Adaptation Syndrome* (G.A.S.) which outlines a process by which our bodies attempt to maintain homeostasis as they navigate and adjust to the constant changes that occur in and around us. Equally important, Selye supports the concept that stress is a part of life. In his classic book, *The Stress of Life* (1956), he states:

> No one can live without experiencing some degree of stress all the time. You may think that only serious disease or intensive physical or mental injury can cause stress. This is false. Crossing a busy intersection, exposure to a draft, or even sheer joy are enough to activate the body's stress mechanism to some extent. Stress is not even necessarily bad for you; it is also the spice of life, for any emotion, any activity causes stress. But, of course, your system must be prepared to take it. The same stress which makes one person sick can be an invigorating experience for another.
>
> It is through the *General Adaptation Syndrome*, or G.A.S., that our various internal organs—especially the endocrine glands and the nervous system—help us both to adjust to the constant changes which occur in and around us

and to navigate a steady course toward whatever we consider a worthwhile goal (Selye, *The Stress of Life*, 1956).

The General Adaptation Syndrome (G.A.S.) is a predictable sequence of reactions that organisms show in response to stressors. This sequence consists of three stages: the Alarm Stage, the Resistance Stage, and the Exhaustion Stage.

Stage I:

Alarm—When there is emotional arousal and the defensive forces of the body are prepared to fight or flee.

Stage II:

Resistance—When there are intense physiological efforts to either resist or adapt to the stressor.

Stage III:

Exhaustion—Occurring if the organism fails in its efforts to resist the stressor.

The research of Richard Lazarus, another prominent expert, offers a perspective on stress that suggests, "it is not the stressor itself that causes stress, but a person's perception of the stressor (Wood, Wood and Boyd, *Mastering the World of Psychology*, page 295, 2004)." Consequently, in an effort to cope with various life stressors, individuals engage in a cognitive process of primary and secondary appraisals of life situations.

Primary Appraisal—an evaluation of the meaning and significance of the situation—whether its effect on one's well-being is positive, irrelevant, or negative.

There are potential outcomes of an individual appraising an event as stressful:

1. Harm or loss (damage that has already occurred)
2. Threat (the potential for harm or loss)
3. Challenge (the opportunity to grow or gain)

Secondary Appraisal—if people judge the situation to be within their control, they evaluate available resources:

- Physical (health, energy, stamina)
- Social (support network)
- Psychological (skills, morale, self-esteem)
- Material (money, tools, equipment)

(Wood, Wood and Boyd, *Mastering the World of Psychology*, page 295, 2004)

The concepts of Selye and Lazarus (briefly noted above), on stress, are encompassed in the holistic perspective of *The Seven Laws of Stress Management*. Foremost, the mental capacity of humans is recognized as a very powerful source for creating positive thoughts (as well as negative thoughts) and for sustaining positive energy throughout our lives. Secondly, each concept is rooted in the belief that there is an ongoing interplay between mind, body and spirit in which we constantly perceive and interpret the events of our everyday lives. Most importantly, our ability to cope with life stressors is a reflection of the level (or degree) of self-awareness and self-understanding we have attained as evidenced by the ability to consistently access available internal and external resources, as needed, to maintain a sense of balance and well-being. *The Seven Laws of Stress Management* seeks to integrate these concepts with its holistic framework by providing you with a comprehensive and systematic approach to develop the self-awareness, self-understanding and discipline necessary to achieve and maintain a sense of balance and well-being in your personal and professional life.

PART I

THE 7 LAWS OF STRESS MANAGEMENT

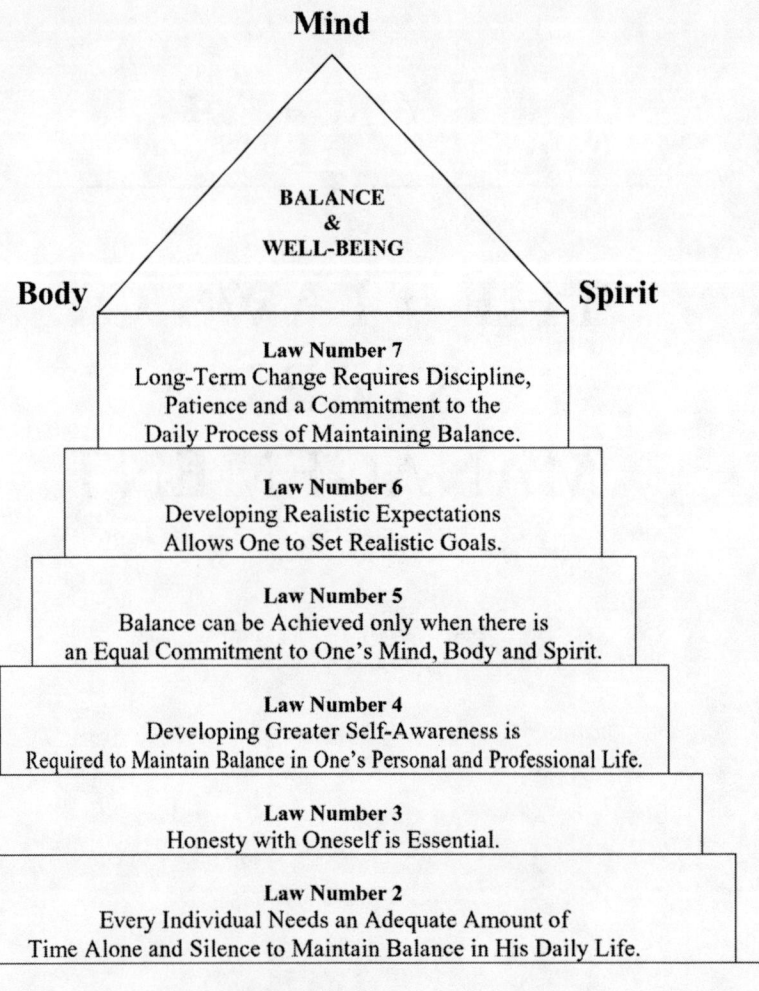

Mind

Body — BALANCE & WELL-BEING — Spirit

Law Number 7
Long-Term Change Requires Discipline,
Patience and a Commitment to the
Daily Process of Maintaining Balance.

Law Number 6
Developing Realistic Expectations
Allows One to Set Realistic Goals.

Law Number 5
Balance can be Achieved only when there is
an Equal Commitment to One's Mind, Body and Spirit.

Law Number 4
Developing Greater Self-Awareness is
Required to Maintain Balance in One's Personal and Professional Life.

Law Number 3
Honesty with Oneself is Essential.

Law Number 2
Every Individual Needs an Adequate Amount of
Time Alone and Silence to Maintain Balance in His Daily Life.

Law Number 1
Stress Management is a Lifestyle that Requires an Individual to be
Proactive Rather than Reactive.

Law Number 1: Stress Management is a Lifestyle that Requires an Individual to be Proactive Rather than Reactive

Stress
is a part
of Life
as we maneuver our way
through
the demands
of work, play
and companionship—

such a delicate balance
we strive to attain.

But, once achieved,
it so easily
seems to quietly
slip away.

This is the dance
that we must Learn
to Love
to Dance.

To constantly perceive
the near future
as one less fulfilling
if we fail
to do in this moment
what we know
must be done
to maintain balance in our lives.

> by Anthony D. Parnell

Each day marks a new opportunity to develop and implement a proactive stress management plan. The first step is to commit yourself to the process of creating and maintaining a lifestyle of healthy habits mentally, physically and spiritually. This pertains to your diet, exercise habits, social interactions, sleep patterns, leisure activities and so forth. Developing a written plan is just as important as the need to sustain consistency in performing the activities in your daily life that promote well-being. When we are committed to approaching each and every day as an opportunity to regain balance and to re-center oneself, over time we develop the discipline necessary to maintain a sense of balance and well-being.

Personal Reflection on Law Number 1

Law Number 2: Every Individual Needs an Adequate Amount of Time Alone and Silence to Maintain Balance in His Daily Life

Silence
is like water.

It is essential
to the body.

But, we usually
never get as much
of it
as we need....

Unless it becomes
a part of our

Daily Ritual
to Rise in Silence,
to Prepare Ourselves to Sleep
in Silence;

To take time
in the Middle of The Day
to Rejuvenate Ourselves
with Silence & Meditation.

We, then, fail to become
that which we
once so greatly desired.

by Anthony D. Parnell

The ability to fully embrace silence (for many individuals) requires a process of overcoming feelings of fear or discomfort with being alone. This is a very difficult process for many, because they have expended more time and energy over the years running from and avoiding the vulnerability of silence and stillness than practicing how to be in tune with their mind, body, and spirit. Or, they have allowed themselves to become drowned by the demands and activities of their daily life which never seems to provide a sufficient opportunity for personal reflection and meditation.

You, then, have to create the opportunity for silence and time alone first by simply committing to it five minutes a day. Then, you must determine a set time each day whether it is morning, afternoon or evening at home or at work. In committing to five minutes a day of silence and being alone, it is a starting point in learning how to consistently take personal inventory. You will discover that in these sacred moments, you will instinctively begin to evaluate, assess and determine the adjustments that must be made in your personal and professional life. You will also discover how calm you have become through your ability to unwind, relax and fully embrace the moment, or how anxious and imbalanced you have become in your daily life by your eagerness to race off to the next activity of the day.

The amount of silence and time needed to maintain a sense of balance and well-being varies with each individual. Only you can decide how much time alone and time in silence you actually need to maintain a sense of balance and well-being. What is most important is that you begin to understand that to adequately address your mental, physical and spiritual needs, you must make time to be alone in silence on a consistent, daily basis.

Personal Reflection on Law Number 2

Law Number 3: Honesty with Oneself is Essential

The Truth
of who I am
remained a mystery

Until I no longer
could bare the
disappointment, the sadness
of finding myself
in the same
emotional and physical
rut—time and time
again.

I finally said to myself
that I truly am ready
for change, lasting
change …

And, then, the realest;
the truest parts
of who I am
were shadows

no longer.

                    by Anthony D. Parnell

Honesty with yourself is essential because life's demands take their toll on mental, physical and spiritual well-being. Because of the inevitable fact that stress is a part of life, adjustments have to be made to maintain a sense of balance personally and professionally. However, adjustments can not be made if you do not possess a level of self-awareness that will enable you to respond accordingly to challenging life situations.

Learning to be honest with yourself goes hand in hand with learning to effectively cope with life situations. This includes accepting personal limitations. You cannot be all things to all people. You cannot be all places at once. You cannot be friends with everyone. Ultimately, in being honest with yourself, your ability to effectively cope with life situations is a combination of doing everything within your power to help yourself, while also remaining open to emotional support from others.

Personal Reflection on Law Number 3

Law Number 4: Developing Greater Self-Awareness is Required to Maintain Balance in One's Personal and Professional Life

Sometimes,

motivation must come
solely from within.

Sometimes,

there is
no other inspiration

except our intense desire,
a deep yearning
for much more
to be revealed
about the essence
of who we really are;

and to feel a sense of peace
and clarity
about the meaning
and the quality
of our lives.

~

A man
who believes that
there is no room
for greater growth
in his life
is a man
who has died a
silent death.

He is a walking
Zombie
though he speaks articulately
and Smiles and Laughs
until left alone.
It is when
he is confronted
with continuous moments of silence,

that his true discontentment
is revealed.

by Anthony D. Parnell

To instinctively know when you are emotionally, physically and mentally worn down resides within you. It simply needs to be discovered and nurtured. You must make it a priority to be still and to re-center yourself when you are feeling overwhelmed, instead of trying to keep up with life's increasing demands.

The commitment to spend a minimum of five minutes a day alone in silence and/or writing is an excellent initial goal for taking self-inventory. Additionally, Appendix A provides a range of self-assessment/self-inventory questions that will help you begin the process of becoming more in tune with your mind, body and spirit, and will help you identify healthy coping strategies for maintaining a sense of balance and well-being (personally and professionally).

Personal Reflection on Law Number 4

Law Number 5: Balance Can be Achieved Only When There is an Equal Commitment to One's Mind, Body and Spirit

"The Balance of One"

The Mind.

The Body.

The Spirit

are One.

Each
as intricately connected

to the other
as branches on a tree.

Though much more than
the physical make-up
of my being

I am much more
than pure intellect.

For, it is my
spiritual nature
that provides the roots
of my existence.

I, then, must nourish
all elements
of who I am

to maintain
the continuity

of the Oneness
of my being.

                      by Anthony D. Parnell

There is an inherent sense of harmony that exists between mind, body and spirit. Much of your daily activity and existence as a human being is intended to be dedicated to sustaining this natural sense of harmony. Mirroring nature itself, you internally embody natural processes. By engaging these natural processes and higher states of existence, you can generate increasing levels of energy and momentum that perpetuate themselves.

In order to tap into this hidden source of energy and wisdom, you must first shift your thinking from a one-dimensional perspective to a holistic perspective. Another significant step is identifying and reexamining your dominant beliefs about wholeness, balance and well-being. But, what are beliefs? Beliefs are "what one has come to think of as truth and what one perceives as reality (*Healing through Writing*, page 37)."

In other words, to begin to view yourself and your life more holistically, you must adopt the belief we, as humans, are spiritual as well as physical and intellectual; that there is a greater and deeper meaning and purpose to our existence that extends beyond simply accumulating material possessions and defining ourselves by social status.

It also requires us to understand and accept that a holistic perspective of balance and well-being is representative of our internal, as well as external condition. Therefore, a person who tends to his physical needs but disregards his mental and spiritual needs has not truly attained a sense of balance and well-being. The same is true of individuals who focuses exclusively on achieving balance in their professional lives, but neglect their personal lives. In adopting new beliefs about the holistic connection between mind, body, and spirit, you will be compelled to more actively and more deeply explore all aspects of your multi-dimensionality.

Personal Reflection on Law Number 5

Law Number 6: Developing Realistic Expectations Allows an Individual to Set Realistic Goals

Step-by-Step

I move toward my goal
as time has become my ally
rather than my foe.

I understand that
where I want to be
tomorrow
begins with
what I do today.

My sense of success
is measured
mostly by

having positive feelings
about who I am
as a person
and learning to accept
myself
for where I am

at this stage of
my Life.

Because I have let go
of my disappointments
and failures of the past,

I can set realistic
goals for my future.

by Anthony D. Parnell

Step-by-Step goals may include key areas such as: Spiritual, Relationship, Financial and Career. The excerpt below taken from *Healing through Writing* (page 30) reinforces the value and benefit of utilizing Step-by-Step goals, to not only set realistic goals, but to set realistic expectations about stress management in general. This is because we often have to be reminded that the goal or desire to completely eliminate stress from our lives is an unrealistic expectation. Stress will always be present in your personal and professional life to some degree. Therefore, the shift in your thinking from "eliminating" stress to learning how to effectively "manage" stress creates a much broader range of possibilities with regards to implementing an effective stress management plan.

> I refer to these goals as Step-by-Step Goals because the emphasis of the exercise is placed on outlining how one can accomplish his or her goals 'step-by-step' within given timelines. The greatest benefit is that one is able to focus on taking small steps in accomplishing one's long-term goals as opposed to placing too much emphasis on accomplishing one's ultimate goal all at once. In other words, Step-by-Step Goals force one to take small steps and to be patient with the process of focusing on one's growth and development one day at a time. A second benefit is that, in establishing increments, one is more inclined to set realistic goals because one can more objectively view what is required to achieve one's long-term goals. This includes the flexibility that is provided in developing Step-by-Step Goals as one is able to change the timelines with regards to ensuring that goals are based upon realistic expectations. A final benefit is that one can feel a sense of accomplishment with successfully completing each small goal. Having opportunities to be rewarded more frequently for some is essential in their maintaining their motivation.

SAMPLE STEP-BY-STEP GOAL RECREATION/EXERCISE

TODAY
I will jump rope for one minute.

THIS WEEK
I will jump rope for one minute every other day.

THIS MONTH
Week 2—I will jump rope for two minutes every other day.

Week 3—I will jump rope for two minutes and do fifty push-ups every other day.

Week 4—I will jump rope for two minutes and do fifty push-ups every other day.

3 MONTHS
I will jump rope for five minutes and do one hundred push-ups every other day.

6 MONTHS
I will jump rope for eight minutes and do 150 push-ups every other day.

1 YEAR
I will jump rope for ten minutes and do 200 push-ups every other day.

Personal Reflection on Law Number 6

Law Number 7: Long-Term Change Requires Discipline, Patience and a Commitment to the Daily Process of Maintaining Balance

Each Day
that I rise
is another day
that I move closer
to being
all that I was meant
to be.

While I have learned
to be patient

with the process
of becoming
a greater me,

I now Understand
that learning to maintain
Decluttered Thoughts and Emotions
and a Decluttered Environment
are critical steps
in learning
to exercise the discipline
required to maintain
balance and well-being
in my daily life.

        by Anthony D. Parnell

Your ability to maintain a healthy lifestyle that promotes balance and well-being is a step-by-step process that is not developed overnight. It requires a daily commitment to personal growth and maintaining balance despite the challenges and obstacles encountered in your personal and professional life. In fully committing yourself to this process, you will begin to develop discipline in your thought patterns and other daily habits, such as the physical care of your body and the decluttering of your thoughts and your environment.

The daily or consistent ritual of being alone in silence, writing and visualizing a balanced personal and professional life is also required to constantly reinforce positive thinking and to maintain emotional equilibrium. Though we all require some degree of participation in specific activities that provide a healthy release for the buildup of negative energy, some individuals are able to maintain a high level of self-awareness and emotional balance without needing to adhere to a strict diet of daily mental and emotional exercises and rituals. However, consistency and patience with oneself and with the process of incorporating various aspects of a holistic stress management plan in one's life are critical components of maintaining a balanced life.

Unfortunately, the concept of "process" is difficult to fully embrace as we have become conditioned to seek and to expect immediate answers and results to most things in life. Regardless of your ability to exercise patience with yourself and the growth process, personal growth, whether physical, spiritual or mental, occurs in stages that are comparable to a continuous cycle of beginnings and endings. Even though some individuals may experience immediate success with implementing an effective stress management plan, over time the discipline exercised in self-awareness and response to mental, physical and spiritual needs in a timely manner will ensure that you do not feel overwhelmed by personal and professional responsibilities.

A graph of the "Stages of Emotional and Spiritual Growth" (an excerpt from *Healing through Writing*, page 64) is illustrated below to serve as a visual reminder of the cyclical process and stages of personal growth.

Stages of Emotional and Spiritual Growth

Denial → Enlightenment\
↕ ↕ →Personal Responsibility→Transformation
Unconsciousness→Self-Awareness/

Personal Reflection on Law Number 7

Part II

7 Steps to Developing and Implementing an Effective Stress Management Plan

Mind

Body / BALANCE & WELL-BEING \ **Spirit**

Step Number 7
Putting It All Together
(Maintaining an Effective Stress Management Plan)

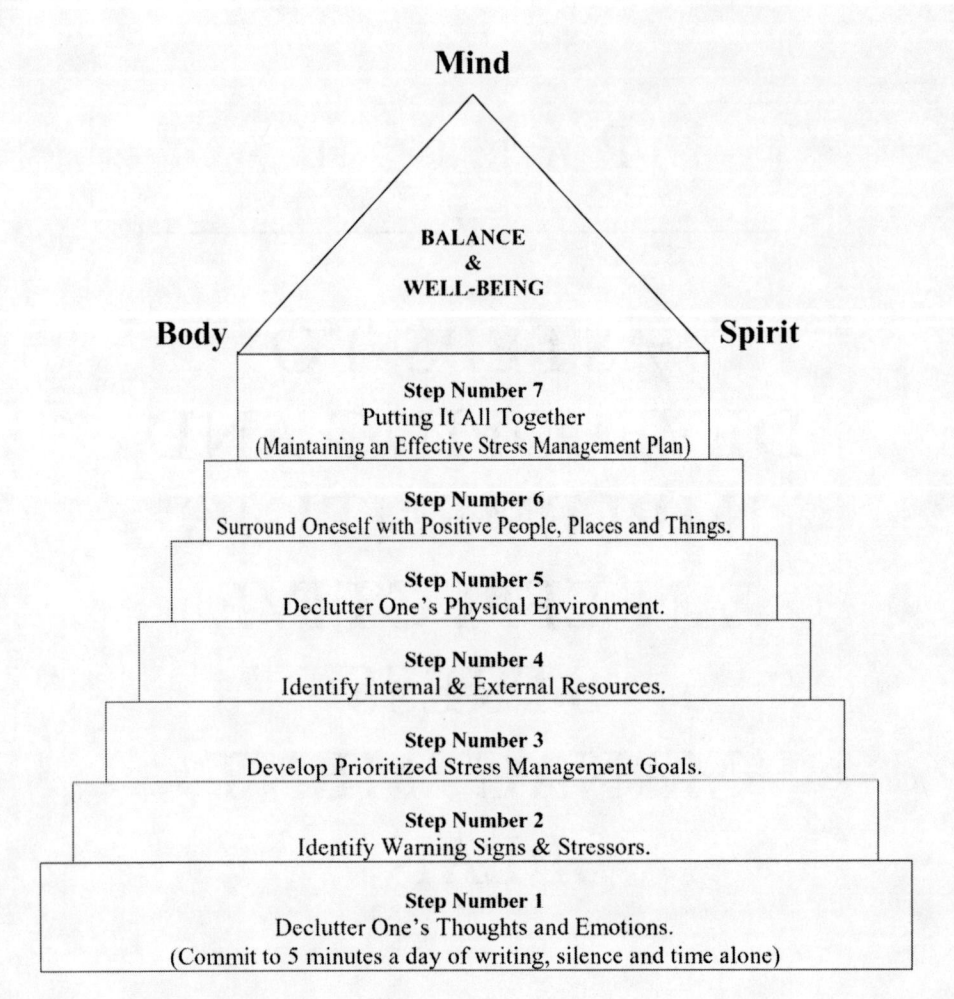

Step Number 6
Surround Oneself with Positive People, Places and Things.

Step Number 5
Declutter One's Physical Environment.

Step Number 4
Identify Internal & External Resources.

Step Number 3
Develop Prioritized Stress Management Goals.

Step Number 2
Identify Warning Signs & Stressors.

Step Number 1
Declutter One's Thoughts and Emotions.
(Commit to 5 minutes a day of writing, silence and time alone)

Step Number 1: Declutter One's Thoughts and Emotions

The stress experienced in daily life frequently comes from feeling that current circumstances are unmanageable. These feelings of helplessness and being overwhelmed are reinforced by seeing piles and piles of paper, and generally speaking, "clutter" in one's physical environment. Yet, in an instant, by simply practicing the decluttering of your thoughts, and your overwhelming feelings, you can suddenly change to feel empowered and light-hearted.

This can be accomplished by writing your thoughts and emotions in a journal or notebook or by even talking to friends. Unfortunately, once your energy has been drained by the increasing demands placed on your time and energy, it can become more and more challenging to find the time and the energy to remove the emotional clutter in your life. Thus, I encourage you to make writing a part of your daily life. As shared earlier, the book *Healing through Writing* discusses this in-depth and provides specific examples on how writing can be utilized as a tool to empower individuals to prevent the build-up of negative energy and emotion and to facilitate personal growth.

The ability to exercise discipline in one's commitment to writing daily, or on a consistent basis, can take time to develop. Writing requires effort, focus, and discipline. It is therefore, strongly suggested that readers begin with an initial commitment of **five minutes a day for five consecutive days**. This should be a free flowing experience, in which you record any thoughts and emotions that come into your consciousness, whether the ideas can be recorded clearly or not. Selecting a time of day that you feel would be conducive to writing is also important. If you experience difficulty getting started or maintaining a consistent flow, six steps to "Picking Up the Pen" taken from *Healing through Writing* (page 47) is presented below to assist you in relaxing and focusing your writing. This is followed by a chart to record your daily efforts to write for **five minutes a day for five consecutive days**.

Six Steps to Picking Up the Pen

1. Set A Time

That is best for you to concentrate and focus your energy (morning, afternoon, after dinner, before bed, and so on) when you can still recall many of the significant events of the day. My mind is most clear early in the morning or late at night. Whenever you decide to set it, make sure you give ample time to unwind and transition from your previous activity. For instance, instead of trying to immediately write, take a few moments to pause and reflect on recent events. This may prove beneficial in providing some initial sense of organization to your thoughts and emotions.

2. Choose a Comfortable Location to Write

Think of a relaxing environment in which you are not likely to be interrupted or distracted. Also, consider a location in your home or office where you feel the greatest sense of peace or positive energy.

3. Set The Mood

Once you have set a time and located a comfortable, relaxing environment, you will have to determine whether a certain style of music will be required to set the mood. It is important that both your mind and body are calm and relaxed, enabling you to channel your energy and focus on your inner self. For most beginners, music will be necessary to help them sustain their focus. Even after years of practice and experience, there are still times when it is extremely difficult for me to identify or express my intense emotions without the aid of some music that resonates (with) my mood. The right music for the right mood helps me to relax and become more open to my thoughts and emotions. With practice and time, you will also be able to identify the source of your emotions and express them.

4. Focus On The Music

Sit with your legs folded, close your eyes, and take long, slow, deep breathes to relax your body and clear your mind. As you breathe, inhale through your nose and exhale through your mouth. When inhaling, focus on taking in positive energy and filling your lungs and chest with air. While slowly exhaling, focus on releasing negative energy. Be careful of the pace of your breathing as to not become dizzy. Then ask yourself, "How do I feel?" as you continue taking long, slow deep breaths and gradually become content with silence and stillness. Even if no thoughts come to mind, there is therapeutic value in sitting in silence with your mind and body completely relaxed. Even though you have closed your eyes, begin writing as soon as you become conscious of the thoughts that enter your mind or as you begin to feel emotions surfacing. Be patient with the process, and if you lose your thoughts, simply refocus on the music. Also, remind yourself that this is a process that takes time, especially if there are years of underlying emotion that have not been fully acknowledged or identified.

5. Write for Yourself

Release expectations of others and the urge to judge your emotions. In learning to accept your emotions, you are learning to accept yourself where you are in your process of spiritual growth and self-awareness.

6. Take Small Steps

On a daily basis, celebrate each accomplishment. Congratulate yourself for having the discipline to write, even if for only five minutes, a realistic goal for the first week. Focus on consistency and detail. Remember: With time and practice you will develop the ability to honestly and succinctly express your thoughts and emotions through the healthy medium of writing.

It is now time to make a commitment to writing in your journal or to sit in silence/meditation for **five minutes a day for five consecutive days**. Use the following chart to record your progress. Additional tracking charts are provided in Appendix B.

Sample Tracking Log for Decluttering Thoughts and Emotions

DAY OF THE WEEK	AMOUNT OF TIME
DAY 1	2 MINUTES
DAY 2	2 MINUTES
DAY 3	NO ENTRY
DAY 4	6 MINUTES
DAY 5	10 MINUTES

Reader's Chart

DAY OF THE WEEK	AMOUNT OF TIME
DAY 1	
DAY 2	
DAY 3	
DAY 4	
DAY 5	

Step Number 2: Identify Warning Signs & Stressors

Step Number 2 assesses your level of self-awareness by identifying warning signs and stressors. Simply speaking, stressors can be defined as "that which produces stress" (Hans Selye, *The Stress of Life*, page 78). Stressors can range from illness and environmental factors to financial concerns and the starting of a new job. Warning Signs are physical, emotional, behavioral and cognitive indicators of the negative impact of stress. Identifying Warning Signs and Stressors is critical, in that it challenges you to begin to develop a proactive philosophy to stress management. Equally, it will challenge you to expand the degree of your self-awareness, which will enable a sustainable balance in your personal and professional life.

The identification of Warning Signs and Stressors, subsequently, will serve as a barometer, or starting point, for gauging the fluctuations in your stress levels. It can also monitor a balance in your personal and professional life. Early identification of warning signs and stressors is also critical. The earlier you detect an imbalance, the sooner balance can be restored to your mind, body, and spirit.

Failure to identify warning signs of stress in its early stages has long-term implications for your mental and physical well-being. According to the National Institute for Occupational Safety and Health (NIOSH), "… evidence is rapidly accumulating to suggest that stress plays an important role in several types of chronic health problems especially":

- Cardiovascular Disease (coronary heart disease, stroke, hypertensive heart disease)
- Musculoskeletal Disorders (job stress increases the risk of back disorders)
- Psychological Disorders (mental health problems such as depression and burnout)

(NIOSH *Stress At Work Publication No. 99-101*, pages 10-11)

A brief list of employment and non-employment-related Warning Signs are listed on the following page. **Take a few moments to circle and then record any Warning Signs** that you can immediately identify. Feel free to add to the list any additional Warning Signs or Symptoms that you are able to identify in your personal or professional life.

Early Warning Signs of Job Stress (NIOSH *Stress at Work Publication 99-101*, page 11)

Headache
Sleep Disturbances
Difficulty in Concentrating
Short Temper
Upset Stomach
Job Dissatisfaction
Low Morale

~

Other Examples of Early Warning Signs (Physical, Mental, Emotional, Behavioral)

Irritability
Sleeping Too Much or Too Little
Exhaustion
Weight Gain or Loss
General Aches and Pains
Increased Use of Alcohol or Drugs
Memory Problems
Inability to Relax
Feeling Overwhelmed

~

Reader's List of Warning Signs in Personal and Professional Life

1.

2.

3.

4.

5.

6.

7.

Now that you have identified some of the warning signs of stress, and made a preliminary assessment of the negative impact of stress in your personal and professional life, you now need to clearly identify and name your current personal and professional stressors. A host of environmental and social causative factors can take a toll on your mind, body, and spirit. More specifically, with regards to your work environment, NIOSH identifies six conditions that may lead to job stress: The Design of Task; Management Style; Interpersonal Relationships; Work Roles; Career Concerns; and Environmental Conditions (NIOSH *Stress At Work Publication No. 99-101*, page 9). NIOSH also reports that effectively managing stress in one's work environment requires an active role for the individual as well as the employer. Working in a professional environment that makes a conscious effort to address the emotional needs of workers is essential to minimizing the negative impact of stress. Given that, "Problems at work are more strongly associated with health complaints than any other life stressor—more so than even financial problems or family problems …" the management of organizations can play a vital role in stress prevention in the workplace and an increased sense of balance and well-being among countless individuals (NIOSH *Stress At Work Publication No. 99-101*, page 5). Changes within any organization that are needed to prevent job stress include:

- Ensuring that the workload is in line with workers' capabilities and resources.
- Designing jobs to provide meaning, stimulation, and opportunities for workers to use their skills.
- Clearly defining workers' roles and responsibilities.
- Giving workers opportunities to participate in decisions and actions affecting their jobs.
- Improving communication—reduce uncertainty about career development and future employment prospects.
- Providing opportunities for social interaction among workers.
- Establishing work schedules that are compatible with demands and responsibilities outside the job.

The emphasis of this book is to empower you to make the necessary adjustments within their personal lives and professional environments to maintain a sense of balance and well-being. As outlined above, this is to work with or without ideal support being available from an employer. Additional tools are available in Appendix C and the "Additional Resources" section of this book for organizations or managers who wish to reduce employee stress.

To complete Step Number 2, several common stressors are listed below/on the following page. Upon reviewing the lists of stressors, **circle and then record any stressors** identified in your professional life. If needed, refer to answers from the Self-Exploratory Questions in Appendix A and "Personal Reflections" on any of the Seven Laws in Part I.

Job Stressors (NIOSH *Stress At Work Publication No. 99-101*, page 9)

The Design of Task
Management Style
Interpersonal Relationships
Work Roles
Career Concerns
Environmental Conditions

~

Other Common Stressors

Money
Health/Illness
Relationships
Relocation
Legal Problems

~

Reader's List of Stressors

1.

2.

3.

4.

5.

6.

7.

Now, prioritize the list of stressors based upon the stressors that have the greatest negative impact on your personal and/or professional life (#1, #2, #3 and so on).

Sample Prioritized List of Stressors:

1. Long Hours and Workload
2. Clutter at Home
3. Clutter at Office
4. Limited/Minimal Task Variety in Work Environment
5. Limited Intellectual and Spiritual Stimulation
6. Limited time alone to write, read and reflect/meditate
7. Inadequate Amounts of Exercise
8. Inadequate Amounts of Sleep (staying up late writing)

~

Reader's Prioritized List of Stressors:

1.
2.
3.
4.
5.
6.
7.
8.
9.
10.

The impact of stressors varies from individual to individual. As previously noted, developing self-awareness is the key to regularly gauging the positive and negative impact of stress in your life. There are also numerous tools for measuring stress levels, and common indicators such as cholesterol and blood pressure levels. It is strongly recommended that physicians or health professionals be consulted in addition to incorporating the philosophy and techniques of *The Seven Laws of Stress Management*. Further, if you are experiencing extreme difficulty performing normal tasks or coping with home or work, it is also strongly recommended that a mental health professional be consulted in addition to utilizing the techniques and philosophy of *The 7 Laws of Stress Management*. The "Additional Resources" section of this book provides professional referral information as well as sources for more detailed information on stress and other health related questions.

Step Number 3: Develop Prioritized Stress Management Goals

You may already enjoy extracurricular and leisure activities that you regularly participate in to maintain a sense of balance and to minimize stress. Healthy extracurricular and leisure activities are valuable resources for minimizing stress in your personal and professional life. These activities or hobbies serve to minimize stress because you find them fun and relaxing. They don't take energy from you. Instead, these activities energize you. It is important to first identify extracurricular and leisure activities that energize you, before beginning to incorporate your stressors and warning signs identified and recorded in Step Number 2 into a formal stress management plan.

Take a few moments to list any important extracurricular or leisure activities beneficial to regularly engage with as a means of minimizing stress in your personal and professional life (e.g. walking, talking, spending quality time with friends, physical exercise and so on).

Example:

> Playing basketball; Watching NBA basketball; Reading biographies on the lives of great people; Watching interviews or biographies on television of prominent entertainers, musicians, actors, businessmen and political figures (Charlie Rose, Tavis Smiley, Bravo Channel); Watching comedy and nature shows on the Discovery Channel, PBS and A&E; Spending time at the ocean or near water; Traveling; Live Entertainment (Jazz Music); Massage Therapy

Reader Extracurricular and Leisure Activities:

_____
_____
_____
_____
_____
_____

Consider which activities are the most enjoyable and the most effective in minimizing stress and the build up of negative energy in your personal and professional life. Prioritize your list of Extracurricular and Leisure Activities (numbering #1, #2, #3 and so on).

An Example of Prioritized Stress Deterrents:

1. Spending Time Alone in Silence (meditating or journaling/writing)
2. Engaging in deeply intellectual conversations about spirituality or life in general
3. Playing basketball
4. Watching NBA basketball
5. Traveling to other cities and countries
6. Spending time at the ocean or near water
7. Playing piano and writing music
8. Reading biographies on the lives of great people
9. Watching interviews or biographies on television of prominent entertainers, musicians, actors, businessmen, political figures (Charlie Rose, Tavis Smiley, Bravo Channel)
10. Watching stand-up comedy acts
11. Watching nature shows on the Discovery Channel, PBS and A&E
12. Watching great drama/suspense films
13. Massage Therapy

Reader's Prioritized Stress Deterrents:

1.
2.
3.
4.
5.
6.

7.
8.
9.
10.
11.
12.
13.

Ask yourself how much time you need to engage in each of these activities on a regular basis to feel a sense of balance and minimize stress. A chart to record the results has been provided on the following page. Appendix D provides additional charts for tracking your progress in incorporating extracurricular and leisure activities into your daily lifestyle.

Sample Extracurricular Activity Chart

ACTIVITY	MINIMUM AMOUNT OF TIME NEEDED TO MAINTAIN BALANCE
1. Spending Time Alone in Silence (meditating or journaling)	1 hour a day
2. Engaging in deeply intellectual conversations about spirituality or life in general	1-3 hours per week (6-8 hours a week)
3. Playing basketball	2-3 days per week for at least 1 hour a day
4. Watching NBA Basketball	1 or 2 games per week (Utilize DVR/TIVO) to record games
5. Traveling	A 3-day weekend out of town every other month; a minimum of 1-2 full weeks a year
6. Spending time alone at the ocean or near the water	1 day per month
7. Playing piano and writing music	4 hours per week
8. Reading biographies on the lives of great people	1 book every 3-6 months
9. Watching interviews or biographies on television of prominent entertainers, musicians, actors, businessmen, political figures (Charlie Rose, Tavis Smiley, Bravo Channel)	4 hours per week
10. Watching stand-up comedy acts or comedy shows/comedy series	2 hours per week

11. Watching nature shows on the Discovery Channel, PBS and A&E	2 hours per week
12. Watching great drama/suspense films	2 hours per week
13. Massage Therapy	1-2 times per month for 1 hour

Reader Extracurricular Activity Chart

	ACTIVITY	MINIMUM AMOUNT OF TIME NEEDED TO MAINTAIN BALANCE
1.		
2.		
3.		
4.		
5.		
6.		
7.		
8.		
9.		
10.		
11.		
12.		
13.		

Now, having identified and prioritized the primary stressors in your personal and professional life, in addition to determining extracurricular and leisure activities that can help in minimizing the negative impact of stress, you are ready to begin the process of developing specific, concise stress management goals related to each primary stressor. This will be accomplished by writing an "I will ..." statement for each of the three primary stressors.

As a visual reminder, list your three primary stressors from Step Number 2:

1. Hours and Workload
2. Clutter at Home
3. Clutter at Office

Select any of the three primary stressors to begin writing your first goal statement. Then, after writing a Goal Statement for each the three primary stressors, prioritize the goal statements (#1, #2, #3 and so on). Even though your first instinct may be to select the greatest stressor for recording Goal Statement #1, in many instances, your initial emphasis should be placed on the goal statement that is easiest to accomplish. As emphasized with Step-by-Step Goals in Law #6, the reason for this recommended strategy is to support your effort to feel a more immediate sense of accomplishment and to avoid feeling defeated because of difficulty or inability to make progress in accomplishing a goal.

When writing an "I will ..." goal statement, focus on incorporating each of the Stressors with previously recorded Leisure/Extracurricular Activities that you feel will adequately counteract or neutralize the negative impact of the stressor.

Example:

Primary Stressor #1: Long Hours at Work and Workload

Goal Statement #1: I will reduce the numbers of hours I work per week by leaving work at 4pm at least one day a week (Monday—Friday) to play basketball for a minimum of 1 hour, by staying at work no later than 7pm or 8pm every night, and by playing at least one hour of basketball on Saturday or Sunday.

Alternative Goal Statement #1: I will jog for 30 minutes Mondays and Thursdays at 6am before going to work to ensure that I have an outlet for releasing aggression and tension that builds up from working long hours at work.

The process continues by recording a Goal Statement for Prioritized Stressor #2, #3 and so on. However, the recommendation is to initially record a maximum of three goal statements. No more than one goal statement should be implemented per week. Once you have developed the discipline to incorporate your first three prioritized goals into your daily lifestyle, then additional goal statements can be added **(see Appendix E)**. Through the examples provided below, implement your stress management goals by following the outlined sequence of:

Primary Stressor #1: Long Hours at Work and Workload

Goal Statement #1: I will reduce the numbers of hours I work per week by leaving work at 4pm at least one day a week (Monday—Friday) to play basketball for a minimum of 1 hour, by staying at work no later than 7pm or 8pm every night, and by playing at least one hour of basketball on Saturday or Sunday.

~

Primary Stressor #2: Clutter at Home

Goal Statement #2: I will schedule Saturday mornings at 11am as my weekly time to declutter my office space at home.

~

Primary Stressor #3: Clutter in Office

Goal Statement #3: I will schedule Monday mornings at 8am and Thursday mornings at 8am as my weekly times to declutter my office at work.

Sample Stress Management Goals Chart

WEEK #1

	SUN.	MON.	TUE.	WED.	THU.	FRI.	SAT.
GOAL #1: I will reduce the numbers of hours I work per week by leaving work at 4pm at least one day a week to play basketball for a minimum of 1 hour and at least one hour on Saturday or Sunday.		4pm					Yes

WEEK #2

	SUN.	MON.	TUE.	WED.	THU.	FRI.	SAT.
GOAL #1: I will reduce the numbers of hours I work per week by leaving work at 4pm at least one day a week to play basketball for a minimum of 1 hour and play at least one hour on Saturday or Sunday.		4pm		4pm			Yes

GOAL #2: I will schedule Saturday mornings at 11am as my weekly time to declutter my office space at home.								Yes-30 Minutes

WEEK #3

	SUN.	MON.	TUE.	WED.	THU.	FRI.	SAT.
GOAL #1: I will reduce the numbers of hours I work per week by leaving work at 4pm at least one day a week to play basketball for a minimum of 1 hour and at least one hour on Saturday or Sunday.	Yes		4pm			4pm	
GOAL #2: I will schedule Saturday mornings at 11am as my weekly time to declutter my office space at home.	No						No
GOAL #3: I will schedule Monday mornings at 8am and Thursday mornings at 8am as my weekly times to declutter my office at work.		Yes			No		

Reader Stress Management Goals Chart

WEEK #1

	SUN.	MON.	TUE.	WED.	THU.	FRI.	SAT.
GOAL #1:							

WEEK #2

	SUN.	MON.	TUE.	WED.	THU.	FRI.	SAT.
GOAL #1:							
GOAL #2:							

WEEK #3

	SUN.	MON.	TUE.	WED.	THU.	FRI.	SAT.
GOAL #1:							
GOAL #2:							
GOAL #3:							

Step Number 4:
Identify Internal and External Resources

A car may be perfectly built, but it still must receive regular maintenance and check-ups to ensure that it performs at optimal levels. Whether or not an individual has been adequately trained in vehicle maintenance and road performance, once the keys have been handed to the driver, the driver then becomes responsible for the performance and the maintenance of the vehicle.

Some drivers possess unique talents and innate abilities so that they become very good drivers in a short amount of time. Others, though having participated in driver's education and endured the rigors of obtaining a driver's license, will still lack the confidence to operate the vehicle safely without fear of wrecking the vehicle.

The analogy of the car is comparable to the Internal and External Resources we possess as we attempt to navigate our way through the maze of life's challenges, obstacles and adversity. Some individuals are blessed with tremendous health, stamina and adaptive abilities and have acquired a wide range of physical, mental and spiritual outlets. The resources of other individuals, while possessing valuable internal and external resources, are underutilized or simply undiscovered. Nevertheless, you possess a particular variety of natural gifts, talents and acquired skills and abilities. Even more, current resources can be strengthened and new resources can be identified and further developed. These strengths and resources can aid you in the process of maintaining balance and well-being.

"Step Number 3" provided an opportunity for you to begin practicing, visualizing and implementing a routine to ensure that balance and well-being are maintained in your personal and professional life. "Step Number 4" will assist you in identifying additional tools and resources that will support your efforts to accomplish each of the Prioritized Stress Management Goals listed in "Step Number 3"; this can also work for future personal and professional goals.

"The ability of an individual to identify and to consistently utilize the Internal and External Resources that have been identified to improve one's life situation and to maintain balance and well-being in one's personal and professional life" was presented as the definition of empowerment at the beginning of this book. With the accomplishment of each Prioritized Stress Management Goal, you will discover more about yourself, while simultaneously learning to more fully appreciate the resources you possess; because with every endeavor in life, an individual must access his or her internal and external resources for daily survival and to fulfill short-term and long-term goals.

Examples of Internal and External Resources are listed on the following page. After taking a few moments to review, **circle any of the Internal and External Resources** listed which you feel you possess. Also, feel free to add any other internal or external resources that are not listed.

INTERNAL RESOURCES

Commitment
Discipline
A Strong Will
Faith—Sense of Spirituality
Time Management (Ability to Prioritize)
Positive Attitude/Positive Mindset
Determination
Courage
Persistence
Self-Confidence
Self-Awareness
Being in Tune with One's Body

~

EXTERNAL RESOURCES

Adequate Transportation
Shelter
Financial Resources to Meet Basic Needs
Social/Emotional Support (Friends, Family)
Extracurricular/Leisure Activities
A Gym Membership

Now, having circled the Internal and External Resources which you feel you currently possess:

> What Internal and External Resources do you feel you currently possess that can be utilized to accomplish Goal #1 which was previously recorded in Step #3?
>
> Example:
>
>> Goal Statement #1: I will reduce the number of hours I work per week by leaving work at 4pm at least one day a week (Monday—Friday) to play basketball for a minimum of 1 hour, by staying at work no later than 7pm or 8pm every night, and playing at least one hour of basketball on Saturday or Sunday.
>>
>> Internal and External Resources: I have a gym membership at 24-Hour Fitness that I can use to play basketball to minimize the potential stress of work overload. I have adequate transportation.
>
> Reader:
>
>> Goal Statement #1:
>>
>>
>> Internal and External Resources:

What additional Internal and External Resources do you feel you need to develop or obtain to assist you in accomplishing Goal #1?

What Internal and External Resources do you feel you currently possess that can be utilized to accomplish Goal #2?

    Goal Statement #2:

    Internal and External Resources:

What additional Internal and External Resources do you feel you need to develop or obtain to assist you in accomplishing Goal #2?

What Internal and External Resources do you feel you currently possess that can be utilized to accomplish Goal #3?

Goal Statement #3:

Internal and External Resources:

What additional Internal and External Resources do you feel you need to develop or obtain to assist you in accomplishing Goal #3?

Step Number 5: Declutter One's Physical Environment

When one first
Declutters his or her
Thoughts and Emotions,
it generally is
much easier
to Declutter one's physical environment.

However, for some,

Decluttering one's physical environment
immediately makes one feel lighter.

But, just as it is recommended
to begin with 5 minutes
a day of journaling,

the same is true of Decluttering
one's Physical Environment.

Begin with small steps
to ensure consistency
and forward progress.

by
Anthony D. Parnell

The stress experienced in daily life frequently comes from feeling that the current circumstances of life are unmanageable. Feelings of helplessness and being overwhelmed can easily be reinforced by seeing piles and piles of paper, otherwise referred to as clutter in one's physical environment. Likewise, in an instant, one's feeling of being overwhelmed can suddenly be transformed to a feeling of being empowered and light-hearted when clutter is removed from one's physical environment.

Unfortunately, once you begin to experience emotional and physical fatigue, your energy is zapped by the constant bombardments that interfere with keeping pace with the increasing demands placed on your time and energy. It can become even more challenging to find the time and the energy to remove the piles of clutter that have accumulated in your physical environment. For this reason, it is very important to maintain a commitment to removing the physical clutter in your physical environment on a consistent or daily basis.

The same approach to decluttering your thoughts and emotions, as outlined in "Step Number 1," needs to be utilized when contemplating how and where to begin in "Decluttering One's Physical Environment;" and, just as piles of clutter accumulate over time, it must be understood that a significant amount of time will also be required to declutter your physical environment. Therefore, it is strongly recommended that you begin by committing to Decluttering One's Physical Environment for Five Minutes a Day for Five Consecutive Days.

Initially, this will allow you to feel an immediate sense of personal accomplishment. Secondly, as shared earlier in Law # 6 ("Developing Realistic Expectations Allows One to Set Realistic Goals"), it will ensure that you set realistic expectations in an effort to restore a sense of open space and positive energy in your physical environment.

The physical presence of family, friends or a professional organizer to assist you, when feeling overwhelmed by physical clutter, may be the only exception to beginning with more than Five Minutes A Day. Otherwise, do not overexert yourself in an attempt to accomplish too much too soon. Rather, be content with taking small steps to achieve some sense of forward progress. And, as you begin to gain confidence and to feel revitalized, slowly increase the amount of time spent each day decluttering your physical environment.

It's easy to understand why some individuals would argue that the most important area to begin decluttering is the area that has the greatest amount of clutter or that causes the greatest amount of stress in one's life. I, however, recommend selecting a room or area in your home or office that is the least stressful or the easiest to declutter so as to quickly feel a sense of confidence. Then, once you have been successful in removing clutter from one room or area, continue to apply the same strategy one room or area at a time. Equally important, once the home or work environment has been completely decluttered, it is vital that you commit to a set time, for a minimum of 15-30 minutes, at least one or two days a week to declutter your physical environment (home and office).

Incorporating a maintenance or prevention plan will ensure that you do not become overwhelmed again by piles of clutter. This requires discipline and an acceptance that maintaining balance is a continuous process.

The philosophy of committing to Five Minutes A Day has even greater relevance because of the reciprocal relationship that exists between decluttering one's thoughts and emotions and decluttering one's physical environment. They directly influence one another. Even though there are some exceptionally gifted individuals who possess the ability to function at high levels with a cluttered physical environment or cluttered thoughts and emotions, this is not true of most individuals. Over time, most individuals are unable to maximize their emotional and spiritual growth and sense of balance and well-being without strengthening these areas. This is due to the fact that, long-term, a person can only spiritually and emotionally evolve to the degree that he or she has been committed to develop the discipline necessary to exercise healthy habits in all aspects of his or her daily life (mentally, physically, personally and professionally).

Gradual steps are required to achieve balance and well-being in your personal and professional life. Consequently, if you are feeling overwhelmed by the clutter that has accumulated in your physical environment, be honest with yourself about how you are feeling. If needed, ask for help from family, or friends, or hire a professional organizer (see "Additional Resources"). Also, reading books on decluttering and personal organizing is another resource that is available.

While some professional organizers are opposed to storing personal belongings and other items until a later date in which there would be adequate time to sort through the items, I personally have used this strategy, on occasion. In doing so, I simply placed piles of cluttered items and belongings that currently were not being utilized into boxes and filing cabinets. Though a temporary solution, this strategy has at times provided me with a sense of relief and an increased ability to concentrate more effectively on the current priorities in my personal and professional life. Simultaneously, it created a greater sense of open space in my physical environment, which made me feel more relaxed and comfortable. Fortunately, I did exercise the discipline to adhere to the date and time I set to return to the piles of clutter in storage and resume the process of decluttering my physical environment.

Charts have been provided below and on the following page for you to record your progress in implementing an initial plan and a maintenance plan for decluttering your physical environment at home or work (also see Appendix F).

However, there are two important questions that you should ask before beginning the actual work of decluttering your physical environment.

1. What time of day is best for you to focus your energy on decluttering your home environment?

2. What room or area of your home or office will you initially focus and concentrate your time and energy on in order to declutter your physical environment?

INITIAL PLAN FOR DECLUTTERING PHYSICAL ENVIRONMENT
(Personal or Professional)

5 MINUTES A DAY	YES	NO
DAY #1		
DAY #2		
DAY #3		
DAY #4		
DAY #5		

MAINTENANCE PLAN FOR DECLUTTERING PHYSICAL ENVIRONMENT
Designated Time: 8am
Designated days per week (2): Monday and Thursday

Sample

Week #1

15-30 MIN-UTES A DAY	Sun.	Mon.	Tue.	Wed.	Thu.	Fri.	Sat.
Day #1 Monday		Yes					
Day #2 Thursday					No		

Week #2

15-30 MIN-UTES A DAY	Sun.	Mon.	Tue.	Wed.	Thu.	Fri.	Sat.
Day #1 Monday		No					
Day #2 Thursday					Yes		

Week #3

15-30 MIN-UTES A DAY	Sun.	Mon.	Tue.	Wed.	Thu.	Fri.	Sat.
Day #1 Monday		Yes					
Day #2 Thursday					Yes		

MAINTENANCE PLAN FOR DECLUTTERING PHYSICAL ENVIRONMENT
Designated Time _____ am/pm
Designated days per week (2): _____

Reader

Week #1

15-30 MIN-UTES A DAY	Sun.	Mon.	Tue.	Wed.	Thu.	Fri.	Sat.
Day #1 _____							
Day #2 _____							

Week #2

15-30 MIN-UTES A DAY	Sun.	Mon.	Tue.	Wed.	Thu.	Fri.	Sat.
Day #1 _____							
Day #2 _____							

Week #3

15-30 MIN-UTES A DAY	Sun.	Mon.	Tue.	Wed.	Thu.	Fri.	Sat.
Day #1 _____							
Day #2 _____							

Step Number 6: Surround Oneself with Positive People, Places and Things

The accumulation of mental, emotional and physical clutter robs an individual of his or her energy and the ability to maintain balance and well-being. To the detriment of many individuals, cluttered relationships can also serve as an additional roadblock to personal growth, balance, and well-being. Yet, few individuals are willing to be completely honest or to carefully examine the negative impact of relationships that take more energy than they give to the individual.

The ability to significantly minimize stress in life is the direct result of the sum of conscious choices made on a daily basis. This includes taking personal inventory periodically, and at critical junctures of your life, to reassess your personal and professional goals, values and beliefs. Learning to set healthy boundaries with family and friends (which encompasses learning how and when to say "no") is a very challenging and painful process. Many individuals compete with intense feelings of guilt when faced with constant requests for time, energy and even money. This is often due to the fact that many live by the belief that they must be willing to sacrifice anything and everything for loved ones no matter the circumstances or the consequences. Yet, without realizing it, an individual may both be blinded by his or her personal beliefs, and fail to realize that family and friends do not share the same values or discipline. Subsequently, they are not willing to make the same sacrifices and compromises in return.

Tremendous effort is required in learning to more readily make distinctions between relationships that drain your energy and those that motivate and inspire you. Self-awareness and honesty with yourself are necessary ingredients. Concurrently, you must recognize and accept that (similar to changing bad habits), you will, over time, develop a set of expectations given past experiences. By expanding your self-awareness and increasing your sense of personal responsibility and discipline, you will more effectively be able to determine the boundaries that are necessary for healthy relationships and learn how to consistently maintain those boundaries once they have been established.

The conscious commitment of an individual to constantly surround his or her self with positive people, places, and things is a defining moment in a life. It is a spiritual milestone, which signifies an attempt to accept complete responsibility for shaping the direction of a life, both personally, and professionally. This defining moment, then, becomes a commitment that will not succumb to social or environmental pressures (i.e. the pressure to buy certain cars, homes, clothes or to befriend or associate oneself with individuals who are not like-minded or like-spirited). Ultimately, it represents a transitional period in life in which an individual gains a renewed sense of clarity about his or her beliefs and values by discovering and fully embracing the courage and strength required to follow his or her own unique path.

Take a few moments to create a list of the positive people, places and things that energize and inspire you. Then, simply make a conscious effort to increase the amount of time you spend surrounded by these positive people, positive places and positive things.

MY PERSONAL LIST OF POSITIVE PEOPLE, POSITIVE PLACES AND POSITIVE THINGS

Step Number 7: "Putting It All Together"

You are to be commended for having navigated your way to the end of this book. Foremost, your sense of self-worth and personal value has been reaffirmed by having read *The Seven Laws of Stress Management*. In reading this book and completing the written exercises, you have strengthened your level of commitment to achieving and maintaining a life of balance and well-being. You have claimed a greater sense of responsibility for your personal growth and for creating the personal and professional life you envision and greatly desire.

The greatest challenge now comes with consistently implementing an effective stress management plan into your daily life. Nevertheless, your anxiety should be minimal. You have been given the necessary tools to be successful in maintaining balance in your personal and professional life. The "Seven Laws," for example, can be reviewed at any time to determine if you are violating any of the laws, which may be limiting your ability to minimize stress. An inventory tool for assessing the impact of your work environment on your level of stress has also been provided. Additionally, "The Seven Steps to Developing and Implementing an Effective Stress Management Plan" can be repeated as many times as needed or when presented with new life challenges such as a job transition, relocation or the loss of a loved one.

Your sustained level of commitment to the "Seven Laws" and the "Seven Steps" is the most essential ingredient to ensuring your success in minimizing stress in your personal and professional life. Overcome any reluctance you may have to referring, as often as needed, to any part of this book in the future.

Utilize the blank charts in the Appendices to continue to record your progress and to create new "Prioritized Stress Management Goals." Even when feeling stuck on one stress management goal or law, take advantage of the opportunity to focus all of your energy on incorporating one goal or one law at a time into your daily life before shifting your attention.

A primary goal of *The Seven Laws of Stress Management* is to serve as a catalyst for you to utilize writing and self-reflection as a tool for maintaining balance and well-being in your personal and professional life. Workshop participants, social work professionals and their clients have successfully utilized and implemented the philosophy and techniques of *The Seven Laws of Stress Management* in their daily lives. It is my hope that by reading this book you have increased your level of self-awareness and already begun to experience decreased levels of stress in your personal and professional life.

"Life's Inner Ocean"

Life's Ocean
flowwwsss
through the Spirit
of man.

the depth
of my soul
reaches the
depth of the ocean.

this is where
my inner peace
is found....

in my soul.

knowing that you are
in the will of
The Divine Universe,
that you have connected
with that deeper
source
of spirituality,
peace and balance.

to see beyond
The Moment.

to see beyond
what physically lies
within my eyesight
and to see spiritually
what is unfolding....

that peace is being found
not in things,

but in Life's Ocean
of Spirit
that flowwwsss
through me.

        by Anthony D. Parnell

Appendix A

Self-Exploratory Questions

Do you recall the happiest time of your life?
If yes, what factors contributed to your feelings of happiness during that period of time?

Have there been any significant changes in your behavior?
If yes, what significant changes have occurred in your behavior?

How long ago do you recall these significant changes occurring in your behavior?

Do you feel that you are living in the past, or the future, or are you fully embracing the moment?

Are your daily thoughts focused on the past or the future rather than on the current moment?

Do you trust yourself to make important decisions?
   If no, when did you begin feeling less confident in your decision-making?

Has there been a significant decline in the number of completed tasks at home or work?
   If yes, when did the decline in the number of completed tasks begin to occur?

Have you experienced a significant decrease in your level of energy?
   If yes, when did you begin to feel a significant decrease in your level of energy?

Is there a consistent or frequent feeling of panic or frustration that you will never be able to catch up—that there are always tasks left unfinished that really need to be completed?

Is there added clutter in your home and/or work environment?

Do friends, relatives or peers constantly tell you that you are stressed?

Are you embarrassed to ask for help to get reorganized?

Appendix B

▼

Maintenance Plan for Decluttering Thoughts

MAINTENANCE PLAN FOR DECLUTTERING THOUGHTS
Designate a time 2 days per week: _____ am/pm

	DAY OF THE WEEK	SUN.	MON.	TUE.	WED.	THU.	FRI.	SAT.
AMOUNT OF TIME								

MAINTENANCE PLAN FOR DECLUTTERING THOUGHTS
Designate a time 2 days per week: _____ am/pm

	DAY OF THE WEEK	SUN.	MON.	TUE.	WED.	THU.	FRI.	SAT.
AMOUNT OF TIME								

Appendix C

Stress in the Workplace Grading Charts

7 KEY ELEMENTS TO ORGANIZATIONAL CHANGE National Institute for Occupational and Safety and Health (NIOSH) Publication No. 99-101 (Booklet "Stress at Work"), (page 15).	GRADE
1. Ensure that the workload is in line with workers' capabilities and resources.	
2. Design jobs to provide meaning, stimulation, and opportunities for workers to use their skills.	
3. Clearly define workers' roles and responsibilities.	
4. Give workers opportunities to participate in decisions and actions affecting their jobs.	

5. Improve communication—reduce uncertainty about career development and future employment prospects.	
6. Provide opportunities for social interaction among workers.	
7. Establish work schedules that are compatible with demands and responsibilities outside the job.	

8 VARIABLES RELATED TO JOB SATISFACTION AND FUNCTIONING EFFECTIVELY IN THE WORKPLACE Albrecht, Karl. *Stress and the Manager: Making it Work for You.* New York: Simon & Schuster, 1979 (page 139).	GRADE
1. Workload	
2. Physical Variables	
3. Job Status	
4. Accountability	
5. Task Variety	
6. Human Contact	
7. Physical Challenge	
8. Mental Challenge	

Appendix D

Weekly and Monthly Extracurricular Activity Chart

WEEKLY EXTRACURRICULAR AND LEISURE ACTIVITIES

	Sun.	Mon.	Tue.	Wed.	Thu.	Fri.	Sat.
1.							
2.							
3.							
4.							
5.							
6.							
7.							
8.							
9.							
10.							

Activity #1 _____

Activity #2 _____

Activity #3 _____

Activity #4 _____

Activity #5 _____

Activity #6 _____

Activity #7 _____

Activity #8 _____

Activity #9 _____

Activity #10 _____

MONTHLY EXTRACURRICULAR AND LEISURE ACTIVITIES

	Jan.	Feb.	Mar.	Apr.	May	June	July	Aug.	Sept.	Oct.	Nov.	Dec.
1.												
2.												
3.												
4.												
5.												
6.												
7.												
8.												
9.												
10.												

Activity #1 _____

Activity #2 _____

Activity #3 _____

Activity #4 _____

Activity #5 _____

Activity #6 _____

Activity #7 _____

Activity #8 _____

Activity #9 _____

Activity #10 _____

APPENDIX E

▼

Stress Management Goals Chart

WEEK #____

	SUN.	MON.	TUE.	WED.	THU.	FRI.	SAT.
GOAL #____:							
GOAL #____:							
GOAL #____:							
GOAL #____:							
GOAL #____:							

Appendix F

Maintenance Plan for Decluttering Environment

PERSONAL MAINTENANCE PLAN
for
DECLUTTERING PHYSICAL ENVIRONMENT

Designated Time: _____ am/pm
Designated days per week (2): _____

Week #1

15-30 MIN-UTES A DAY	Sun.	Mon.	Tue.	Wed.	Thu.	Fri.	Sat.
Day #1 _____							
Day #2 _____							

Week #2

15-30 MIN-UTES A DAY	Sun.	Mon.	Tue.	Wed.	Thu.	Fri.	Sat.
Day #1 _____							
Day #2 _____							

Week #3

15-30 MIN-UTES A DAY	Sun.	Mon.	Tue.	Wed.	Thu.	Fri.	Sat.
Day #1 _____							
Day #2 _____							

PROFESSIONAL MAINTENANCE PLAN
for
DECLUTTERING PHYSICAL ENVIRONMENT

Designated Time: _____ am/pm
Designated days per week (2): _____

Week #1

15-30 MIN-UTES A DAY	Sun.	Mon.	Tue.	Wed.	Thu.	Fri.	Sat.
Day #1 _____							
Day #2 _____							

Week #2

15-30 MIN-UTES A DAY	Sun.	Mon.	Tue.	Wed.	Thu.	Fri.	Sat.
Day #1 _____							
Day #2 _____							

Week #3

15-30 MIN-UTES A DAY	Sun.	Mon.	Tue.	Wed.	Thu.	Fri.	Sat.
Day #1 _____							
Day #2 _____							

APPENDIX G

▼

Self-Care Monitoring Chart

	5 MINUTES ALONE	ADEQUATE AMOUNT OF SLEEP	HEALTHY DIET	EXTRACURRICULAR ACTIVITIES
SUNDAY				
MONDAY				
TUESDAY				
WEDNESDAY				
THURSDAY				
FRIDAY				
SATURDAY				
SUNDAY				
MONDAY				
TUESDAY				
WEDNESDAY				

THURSDAY				
FRIDAY				
SATURDAY				
SUNDAY				
MONDAY				
TUESDAY				
WEDNESDAY				
THURSDAY				
FRIDAY				
SATURDAY				
SUNDAY				
MONDAY				
TUESDAY				
WEDNESDAY				
THURSDAY				
FRIDAY				
SATURDAY				

Notes

Notes

Notes

Additional Resources

Websites:

www.cdc.gov/niosh The National Institute for Occupational Safety and Health (NIOSH) offers more detailed information about job stress. Additionally, NIOSH, as part of the Centers for Disease Control and Prevention (CDC) is the Federal agency responsible for conducting research and making recommendations for the prevention of work-related illness and injury. As part of its mandate, NIOSH works with industry, labor and academia to better understand the stress of modern work, the effects of stress on safety and health, and ways to reduce stress in the workplace. NIOSH can also be contacted by email: **pubstaft@cdc.gov** or by calling 1-800-232-4636.

www.helpguide.org/mental/stress.com A detailed outline of stress warning signs and symptoms (behavioral, cognitive, emotional, and physical) and other health related questions.

www.medicinenet.com A detailed outline of stress warning signs and symptoms and other health related questions.

www.apa.org (American Psychological Association) Information on stress and other health related questions.

www.napo.net (National Association of Professional Organizers) Professional assistance in decluttering and organizing your home and work environment.

Locating a Psychologist or Mental Health Professional in Your Area:

For a list of consultants in your area who specialize in job stress, contact the American Psychological Association (APA) 1-800-964-2000.

For licensed mental health therapists, contact the Board of Behavioral Science Examiners for your state or look in the yellow pages under Mental Health Information, Psychologists and Psychotherapists.

The National Suicide Prevention Lifeline:

A 24-hour, toll-free suicide prevention service available to anyone in suicidal crisis. If you need help, please dial **1-800-273-TALK (8255)**. With over 120 crisis centers across the country, you will be routed to the closest possible crisis center in your area. **www.suicidepreventionlifeline.org**

References

Albrecht, Karl. *Stress and the Manager: Making it Work for You.* New York: Simon & Schuster, 1979.

Gawain, Shakti. *Creative Visualization: Use the Power of Your Imagination to Create What You Want in Your Life.* Berkeley: Nataraj Publishing, 2002.

Goldway, Elliott M., ed. *Inner Balance: The Power of Holistic Healing: Insights of Hans Selye, of Elisabeth Kubler-Ross, of Marcus Bach and others.* Englewood Cliffs, N.J.: Prentice-Hall, 1979.

Murphy, Joseph. *The Power of Your Subconscious Mind.* New York: Bantam Books (Reward Books), 2000.

National Institute for Occupational and Safety and Health (NIOSH) *Stress at Work Publication No. 99-101.* NIOSH, 1995.

National Institute for Occupational and Safety and Health (NIOSH) *Working with Stress Publication No. 2003-114d* [DVD]. NIOSH, 2002.

Orman, Suze. *The Courage to be Rich.* New York: Riverhead Books, 2002.

Orman, Suze. *The Laws of Money: 5 Timeless Secrets to Get Out and Stay Out of Financial Trouble.* New York: Free Press, 2004.

Parnell, Anthony D. *Healing through Writing: A Journaling Guide to Emotional and Spiritual Growth.* Lincoln, NB: iUniverse, 2005.

Selye, Hans. *Stress without Distress.* Philadelphia: Lippincottt, 1974.

Selye, Hans. *The Stress of Life.* McGraw-Hill Book Company, 1956.

Wood, Samuel E., Ellen Green Wood and Denise Boyd. *Mastering the World of Psychology*. Upper Saddle River, NJ: Pearson Education Inc., 2004.

Empowerment Workshops

Anthony D. Parnell, M.S.W. author of *The 7 Laws of Stress Management, Healing through Writing: A Journaling Guide to Emotional & Spiritual Growth, Mind Games* and *In Search of Soul* has developed a series of unique workshops designed to empower you to achieve and maintain balance and well-being in your personal and professional life.

"Stress Management" Workshop

- **Learn 7 simple steps for developing a stress management plan**
- **Identify 7 key laws for maintaining balance in your daily life**
- **Increase productivity in your professional and personal life**

   (Ideal for 1-Hour Lunch Presentations for businesses and organizations)

~

"Time Management" Workshop

- **Improve ability to prioritize daily tasks and responsibilities**
- **Maintain a greater sense of personal and professional organization**
- **Reduce stress and increase productivity in your personal and professional life**

~

"Healing through Writing" Workshop

- Learn about the spiritual and emotional benefits of keeping a daily journal

- Improve your ability to express your thoughts and emotions through writing

- Identify ways to more effectively manage stress

~

To obtain additional information on scheduling a workshop, visit our website or call us at (818) 973-3159:

NT™ **New Thought Management, Inc.**™

www.NewThoughtManagement.com
2202 South Figueroa Street, #232
Los Angeles, CA 90007

978-0-595-45660-4
0-595-45660-X